YOU GOTTA MEET MR. PIERCE!

THE STORIED LIFE OF FOLK ARTIST ELIJAH PIERCE

by **Chiquita Mullins Lee** and **Carmella Van Vleet**

illustrated by **Jennifer Mack-Watkins**

Kokila

Kokila
An imprint of Penguin Random House LLC, New York

First published in the United States of America by Kokila, an imprint of Penguin Random House LLC, 2023

Text copyright © 2023 by Chiquita Mullins Lee and Carmella Van Vleet
Illustrations copyright © 2023 by Jennifer Mack-Watkins

Kokila & colophon are registered trademarks of Penguin Random House LLC.

Visit us online at penguinrandomhouse.com.

Library of Congress Cataloging-in-Publication Data is available.

Manufactured in China

ISBN 9780593406502

1 3 5 7 9 10 8 6 4 2
TOPL

Design by Jasmin Rubero | Text set in Gelica

To Geoff Nelson, who gifted me Pierce's story;
Ursel White Lewis, who gifted the Columbus Gallery with Pierce's
carvings; Bettye Stull and Mimi Chenfeld, who gifted Pierce,
then me, friendship; Carmella, for the journey; and my mother, Dorothy,
who gifted me love of books and faith in God.
—C.M.L.

For my mom, who introduced me to art.
And for Chiquita, who introduced me to Elijah.
—C.V.V.

For Essence, Kaiden, Kurtis, Nana, my father, brothers, friends and
family, supporters, and all the dreamers in the world.
—J.M.W.

CREEEAK!

The screen door announces as Dad and I
walk into Elijah Pierce's barbershop.

"You gotta meet Mr. Pierce!" Dad says.

Wood carvings. They're everywhere! And laughter. Razors and roaring laughter. Scissors and stories. Tonics and tunes on the radio. The barbershop on East Long Street is the place to be!

"Have you heard the news?" Mr. Pierce asks.

While Dad and Mr. Pierce talk about who won the big game, I try to draw a picture. Nothing looks good enough.

Mr. Pierce admires my new pencil set.

"My mother gave me these," I say.

He tells me his daddy gave him a pocket-knife when he was my age. His uncle Lewis taught him to carve.

"I thought a pocketknife was about the best thing I'd ever seen."

COMB
SNIP

Mr. Pierce asks me what I'm working on.
"A picture for my mom," I say.
"You know, I made a house for my mother with all the furniture."
I'm confused, but he explains that he carved her a dollhouse.
"I bet she liked it," I say. "I can't think of anything good to draw."
Mr. Pierce studies my head. Turns it left and right. Up and down.

"When I was about eight or nine, my dog and I would go down to the creek bank, and fish and whittle. I'd pick a tree that had soft bark, maybe beech, and carve anything I could think of. Horses, dogs, and cows . . . anything that came to mind."

"I could see a picture that I liked, or a person would tell me a story; sometimes I'd hear a song or go to church and hear a man preach a sermon . . . and I'd get me a piece of wood and start to carve it."

"Turning stories into art? I never thought of that," I say.

Mr. Pierce laughs. "I never dreamed that it'd ever amount to anything much, but I just like to do it."

SPIN

"Everything I carve, I want it to tell some kind of story," Mr. Pierce says as he motions for me and Dad to follow him.

Art. It's everywhere! Sculptures and walking sticks. Models and message signs. The gallery on East Long Street is something to see!

"Wow! You carved all of these?"

Mr. Pierce nods and grabs a hunk of wood from the box beside him. He studies the wood. Turns it left and right. Up and down.

HONE ROUGH

A carving called *The Place of My Birth* catches my eye.
"Were you really born on a farm in a log cabin?"
"Right out almost in the cotton field."

"My class went on a field trip to a farm once," I tell him. "I love animals. Maybe I could try to draw one."

Mr. Pierce points to a shelf full of animals. "Boys used to come in the shop, say, 'Pierce, here's a horse. Here's a tiger.'—And they would bet me I couldn't carve it. So I'd do everything I could to carve it."

Mr. Pierce carved people, too.
Everyday people.
And famous people.
"That's Hank Aaron! I saw him break
Babe Ruth's homerun record on TV!
Maybe I could draw him."

A walking stick is leaning in
the corner. "That looks like my
grandmother's cane, only fancier."
"The more you look, the more
you see," Mr. Pierce says.
He's right.

"What's happening in this one?"

Mr. Pierce tells us a story about the time he escaped an angry mob hunting for someone accused of a crime. A detective arrested Mr. Pierce and put him in jail because of the color of his skin.

"Finally they sent for someone to identify me. The man looked me up and down and said, 'No . . . He ain't the one . . . ' So they turned me loose."

"That sounds scary," I tell him.

Mr. Pierce says the Lord protected him from that angry mob.

Mr. Pierce shows me something else. "I bet
you've never seen anything like this before!"
"These are Bible stories, aren't they?" I ask.

He nods and tells me it was his wife's suggestion to put the carvings into a giant book. He wasn't sure it was a good idea at first. "But we glued them onto cardboard pages, and now it's the only book of its kind in the world."

"It's for me? Thank you!"

Mr. Pierce smiles. "People say I've given away a fortune, but I enjoy it. I get as much a kick out of giving as they do receiving."

BLESS

On the way out, I tell Dad,
"I think I know what I
want to draw . . ."

A GROUNDBREAKING EXHIBIT

Elijah's work was part of "Black Folk Art in America, 1930–1980." This traveling 400-piece exhibit, which opened in February 1982 at the Corcoran Gallery in Washington, DC, was groundbreaking in many ways. The show marked the first time Black folk artists were included in a major exhibit. It also challenged the art community to start including work from untrained artists and artists of different backgrounds. And it created a higher demand for folk art, which in turn meant artists were paid more for their work.

The show included nineteen of Elijah's carvings, including *Power of Prayer* and *Universal Man.*

ELIJAH PIERCE'S HONORS

1973: Wins first prize in the International Meeting of Naïve Art in Zagreb, Yugoslavia (modern-day Croatia)

1973: Becomes one of the first Black artists to exhibit at Columbus Gallery of Fine Arts (now called the Columbus Museum of Art)

1980: Receives an honorary doctorate from Franklin University in Columbus, Ohio

1982: His work is included in the groundbreaking exhibit "Black Folk Art in America 1930–1980"

1982: Wins a National Endowment for the Arts National Heritage Fellowship

1983: The Elijah Pierce Art Gallery is declared a National Historical Site. (The building was demolished in the late 1980s.)

1984: The Martin Luther King Jr. Performing and Cultural Arts Complex in Columbus, Ohio, names the Elijah Pierce Gallery in his honor

1991: Is inducted into the National Barber Museum Hall of Fame in Canal Winchester, Ohio

2000: A statue of Elijah Pierce is erected on the campus of Columbus State Community College, a few hundred feet west of where his barbershop stood

2014: Is honored on the Long Street Bridge Cultural Wall in Columbus, Ohio

Elijah Pierce (March 5, 1892–May 7, 1984) was born in a log cabin in Baldwyn, Mississippi. His father was a formerly enslaved man named Richard, who loved farming. His mother, Nellie, as well as Elijah's two older brothers and younger sister, loved farming, too. Not Elijah. The minute his chores were done for the day, he took his dog and headed to the nearby woods to carve.

When he was a teenager, Elijah loved to hang around the local barbershop. He learned to cut hair and listened to the men talk about their adventures in the big cities. As a young man, Elijah hopped on a train headed north. He rode the rails around the country, cutting hair and carving wood along the way. He became a preacher in Illinois. And he fell in love with a woman named Cornelia. He followed her to Columbus, Ohio, and they married. Elijah fathered two sons, Arthur and Willie, who remained in Baldwyn.

Cornelia was Elijah's second wife. His first wife, Zetta Palm, passed away shortly before he left Mississippi. He was married to Cornelia for twenty-five years, until her death in 1948. His third wife, Estelle, whom he married when he was sixty years old, encouraged him to keep carving and helped arrange art exhibits.

Elijah once said, "I didn't even know I was an artist until they told me." This sentiment was probably true for many folk and traditional artists of the past. These artists were not always recognized or respected because they weren't formally trained, and because they were often people of color, immigrants, or came from immigrant families. They were craftspeople, considered common, and so was their art. But the National Endowment for the Arts (NEA) sought to change that when they created the National Heritage Fellowship program in 1982. Elijah was one of its recipients that year. Each year since then, the NEA has honored up to fifteen traditional or folk artists for their lifelong excellence and contributions to the cultural arts.

Over his lifetime, Elijah carved thousands of pieces. Often, if someone admired a particular piece, Elijah would give it to them. Especially if he thought the person needed to hear the carving's message.

The *Book of Wood* is Elijah's most famous work of art. It is made up of thirty-three reliefs mounted on seven pages of wood paneling that are two feet tall and three feet wide. This was one of the few woodcarvings Elijah kept for himself while he was alive, declaring it too sacred to part with. It is currently owned by the Columbus Museum of Art.

As he got older, arthritis in his hands made it difficult for Elijah to carve, but he continued to do what he could. And he mentored other artists, including Leroy Almon, Queen Brooks, Kojo Kamau, and Aminah Robinson. As his fame grew, people flocked to his barbershop to see his art. Elijah got a kick out of all the attention. He once slyly told a friend, "You know, I'm famous now. If I'd-a known this all those years ago, I would-a bought a bigger hat."

Following Elijah's death, Estelle helped preserve his legacy by keeping his barbershop art gallery open to the public (until it was sold in 1987) and selling many of his carvings to the Columbus Museum of Art. Today, his art hangs in a number of permanent museum collections and continues to delight others. Most importantly, his work continues to tell his stories. And these stories make up the book of his life.

"Your life is a book and every day is a page."
–Elijah Pierce

© Jeffrey Wolf

Elijah Pierce in his studio, circa 1977

WHERE TO SEE ELIJAH'S WORK

Columbus Museum of Art
(Columbus, Ohio)

American Folk Art Museum
(New York, New York)

High Museum of Art
(Atlanta, Georgia)

Smithsonian American Art Museum
(Washington, DC)

Milwaukee Art Museum
(Milwaukee, Wisconsin)

ELIJAH PIERCE'S ART APPEARING IN THIS BOOK

All images, with the exception of Mr. and Mrs. Hank Aaron, provided by the Columbus Museum of Art.

The Place of My Birth, 1977
Carved and painted wood relief with glitter
29 ⅜ x 27 ⅛ x 1 ⅜ in.
(74.61 x 68.9 x 3.49 cm)
Museum Purchase, 1985.003.074

Donkey, 1972
Carved and painted wood
7 ¼ x 6 ⅜ in. (18.42 x 16.19 cm)
Gift of Mrs. Ursel White Lewis, 1976.004.002

Lion (Date unknown)
Carved and painted wood
7 x 15 x 3 ¼ in. (17.78 x 38.1 x 8.26 cm)
Gift of Mrs. Ursel White Lewis in memory of
Howard W. Lewis, 1995.002

Mr. and Mrs. Hank Aaron, 1974
Wood and paint
19 ½ x 14 ¾ in. (49.53 x 9.08 cm)
High Museum of Art, Atlanta,
gift of Gordon W. Bailey in honor of
Henry "Hank" and Billye Suber Aaron, 2016.42

Tiger, 1972
Carved and painted wood with applied rhinestones
3 ⅝ x 9 ⅛ in. (9.21 x 23.18 cm)
Gift of Mrs. Ursel White Lewis
1976.004.001

Archie Griffin, 1976
Carved and painted wood
16 ⅛ x 14 ⅛ x 3 ⅝ in.
(40.96 x 35.88 x 9.21 cm)
Museum Purchase, 1985.003.010

The Statue of Liberty, 1973
Painted wood relief
28 ⅛ x 14 ⅛ x 1 ⅛ in.
(71.44 x 35.88 x 2.86 cm)
Museum Purchase, 1985.003.087

Dragon, 1972
Carved and painted wood with metal details
4 ½ x 8 ½ x 2 in.
(11.43 x 21.59 x 5.08 cm)
Gift of Gloria K. and James V. Warren
2006.024.007

Elijah Pierce, Woodcarver, (Date unknown)
Painted wood with green and blue marking pen
14 ½ x 24 ⅜ x ¾ in.
(36.83 x 61.91 x 1.91 cm)
Museum Purchase, 1985.003.030

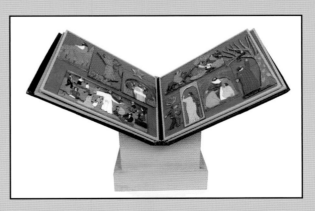

Snake cane, (Date unknown)
Carved and painted wood with rhinestones
38 in. (96.52 cm)
Museum Purchase, 1985.003.084

The Book of Wood, 1932
Carved and painted wood reliefs on wood
paneling
27 ⅛ x 31 x 1 ¼ in.
(68.9 x 78.74 x 3.18 cm)
Museum Purchase, 1985.003.002a-d

ONE FINAL NOTE FROM THE AUTHORS

While the quotes from Elijah in this story are real (taken from various interviews and conversations over the years), the boy in this story is fictional. Because of his arthritis, it is not likely Elijah would've still been cutting customers' hair when this story takes place in the mid to late '70s.

ARTIST'S NOTE

The creation of this book started in 2020, but my connection to the story started when I was a child, growing up during the '90s in my hometown of Goose Creek, South Carolina. I have fond memories of my mother, a former beautician who owned a hair salon and opened a barber shop for my eldest brother, Eric A. Mack. Through the designs he created when cutting hair, he was able to express himself as an artist. I view barbershops as energetic gathering spaces where people in the community can share the latest news, tell funny stories, and exchange advice. I wanted my illustrations to mirror what you would actually see and experience in them, such as posters that line walls, TV screens, laughter, and music in the air. Barbershops have the power to be a safe place for people to uniquely express themselves, where our community is made to feel pampered and each member can feel proud of who they are.

While illustrating this book, these memories, along with research I did to learn more about Elijah Pierce, helped me imagine what it would have been like for his customers to experience his barbershop. I used archival photographs by Jeffrey Wolf and the films *Elijah Pierce: Wood Carver* and *Elijah Pierce Sermons in Wood* by Carolyn Allport. The photographs and films helped me learn more about Mr. Pierce as an artist and showed me how special of a space his barbershop and artist studio were. He was a storyteller, entrepreneur, barber, and self-taught artist. In this book, I created illustrations using the mokuhanga printmaking technique and mixed-media collage. The origins of mokuhanga were developed during the Edo period in Japan, and the earliest forms can be traced back to China and Korea. Historically, the medium of printmaking has been used to document and tell stories of the past and present. As an artist and business owner, I am inspired by Elijah Pierce's story. It motivates me to pursue my own dreams as an artist with an interest in education and children.

© Robin Dreyer

Jennifer Mack-Watkins finishing the art for this book at Penland School of Crafts in 2022